RELIGIONS OF HUMANITY

Chelsea House Publishers
1974 Sproul Road, Suite 400
Broomall, PA 19008

The Chelsea House world wide web address is
www.chelseahouse.com

English-language edition
© 2002 by Chelsea House Publishers, a subsidiary
of Haights Cross Communications
All rights reserved.

First Printing

1 3 5 7 9 6 4 2

Library of Congress Cataloging-in-Publication Data Applied For:
ISBN: 0-7910-6632-0

© 2000 by Editoriale Jaca Book spa, Milan
All rights reserved.

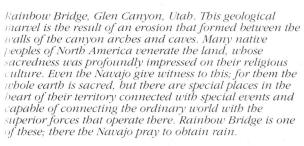

Rainbow Bridge, Glen Canyon, Utah. This geological marvel is the result of an erosion that formed between the walls of the canyon arches and caves. Many native peoples of North America venerate the land, whose sacredness was profoundly impressed on their religious culture. Even the Navajo give witness to this; for them the whole earth is sacred, but there are special places in the heart of their territory connected with special events and capable of connecting the ordinary world with the superior forces that operate there. Rainbow Bridge is one of these; there the Navajo pray to obtain rain.

Originally published by Editoriale Jaca Book, Milan, Italy

Design by Jaca Book

Original English text by Lawrence E. Sullivan

LAWRENCE E. SULLIVAN

THE RELIGIOUS SPIRIT OF
THE NAVAJO

In Monument Valley, two women on the threshold of a "hogan" covered with clay. The "hogan" is the preeminent Navajo construction and it stands as a veritable womb of the cosmic code of these people; its external form and its internal space, in fact, contain the fundamental elements of the Navajo concept of the cosmos.

CHELSEA HOUSE PUBLISHERS
PHILADELPHIA

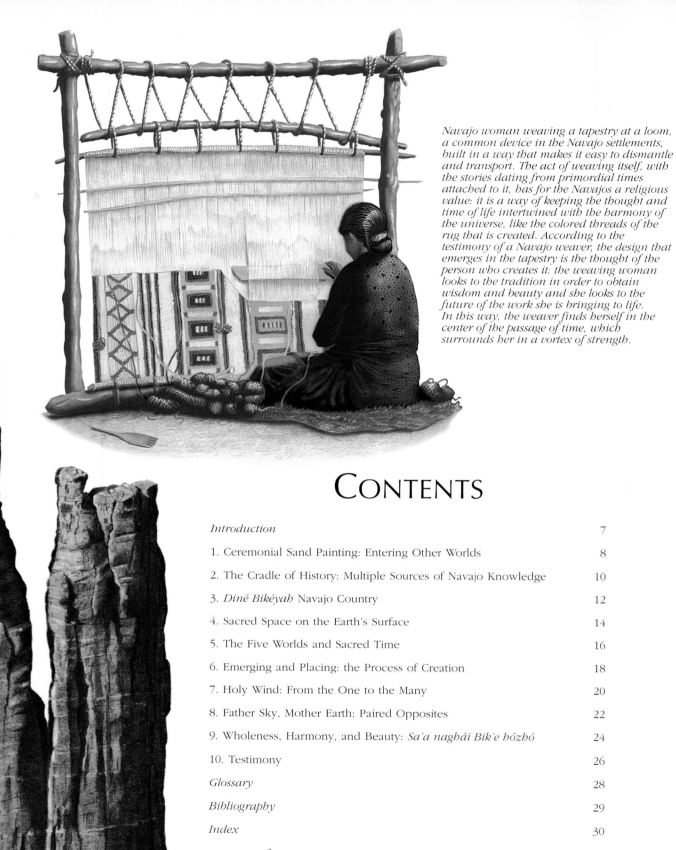

Navajo woman weaving a tapestry at a loom, a common device in the Navajo settlements, built in a way that makes it easy to dismantle and transport. The act of weaving itself, with the stories dating from primordial times attached to it, has for the Navajos a religious value: it is a way of keeping the thought and time of life intertwined with the harmony of the universe, like the colored threads of the rug that is created. According to the testimony of a Navajo weaver, the design that emerges in the tapestry is the thought of the person who creates it: the weaving woman looks to the tradition in order to obtain wisdom and beauty and she looks to the future of the work she is bringing to life. In this way, the weaver finds herself in the center of the passage of time, which surrounds her in a vortex of strength.

CONTENTS

Drawing shows Spider Rock. It is a sandstone formation 130 meters high, situated in the Canyon de Chelly, a location that occupies a special place in the mythology and history of the Navajo. According to the traditional story, the Spider Woman, a character who appears in the stories of the origin of the Navajo people, wove her first cloth from the top of this rock and then taught women to weave; thus, from the beginning, the women among the Navajo took on this task. The Spider Woman taught the women how to design allegorical figures in threads that would remind them of the formation of the stars. The life of humans in fact must be able to relate to the stars, the sun, the animals and every natural element. This serves to maintain order in thought and actions that would otherwise be lost.

INTRODUCTION

Navajo religious life is rich and complicated. Its focus can be found in ceremonies celebrated for and by individuals and communities. These ceremonies renew all those who join in them and are designed to place the Navajo in contact with supernatural beings who possess special knowledge. The goal of these ceremonies is to celebrate life in all its forms. The ceremonies vary greatly. In a way, the ceremonial system is like the corn plant that is so important to Navajo life. The various kinds of ceremonies, like the fruitful branches of the plant, stem out from the main stalk, which is *hózhóójí*, the Blessingway ceremony.

Hózhóójí is especially important at three stages of life: birth, an adolescent girl's coming-of-age ceremony, and the renewal of medicine bundles called *jish*. Blessingway prevents *hóchó* (bad conditions) and wards off misfortune; it ensures health, prosperity, good order, and blessings. In the Blessingway ceremony, a detailed story is told of the mythic underworlds in which all ceremonies are deeply rooted and from which they draw their life. Each of the various ceremonies has its own origin story; they tell of the mythic adventures of the Holy People in those underworlds, and all branch off from the central story of the Blessingway. Some Navajos believe that they will exist only as long as *hózhóójí* (Blessingway) is performed.

Enemyway (*'anaa'jí*), which is performed to counteract harmful contacts with non-Navajos, especially combatants in war, is performed without the use of a ceremonial rattle. (Navajo soldiers who served in the United States armed forces, such as the famous Navajo code-talkers who communicated secret information in their own Navajo language during World War II, were treated with *'anaa'jí* ceremonies when they returned home to Navajo country). Other ceremonies use the rattle. Over the last century, about 50 terms have been used to describe these ceremonies, but the different terms really refer to only 24 ceremonies. Today only 11 ceremonies remain well known to the Navajos, and no more than seven of these are frequently celebrated: Shootingway, Flintway, Mountainway, Nightway, Navajo and Chiricahua Windways, and Hand Tremblingway. They are usually performed according to one of three patterns: Holyway (which restores health to a patient by attracting what is good); Evilway (which sends away evil and harm); and Lifeway (which treats injuries caused by accidents).

Singing is an essential element in the Navajo rituals; it evokes the voice of the wind, which is the most powerful cosmic force. The singer whose knowledge is complex and detailed is also endowed with a series of sacred accessories that emphasize his communicative energy with superior forces. The drawing shows two painted rattles covered with elements from the animal world—horsehair, shammy leather, eagle feathers.

1
CEREMONIAL SAND PAINTING: ENTERING OTHER WORLDS

Imagine that a young girl is sick. Her family has arranged a chantway ceremony to rebuild her strength. The *hataalii*, or ceremonial singer, guides the community in performing special sounds and movements around her. The ceremony lasts several days. At first, the singer and his helpers pray and ready themselves. He prepares the girl, her family and other participants by telling them what to eat, how to behave, and what steps they must take to purify themselves. During the early days of the ceremony, the patient rests. She washes in hot steam baths with soap made from special plants and eats from ceremonial food containers. These actions begin to fill her and the community with healing power.

The community participates by praying, singing, dancing, playing rattles or drums, and dressing in special outfits designed to call to mind supernatural beings. On the final day of the ritual, the ceremony lasts all night. Around the *hogan*, the special house where the ceremony is being held, the singer places powerful objects such as jewels, crystals, feathers, and hollow reeds containing tobacco and moist pollen. These beautiful objects attract the healing powers they represent. The singer's chant breathes life into them, recalling how the objects gained their power in the first place and how they came into the possession of human beings. When all is ready, the singer and his assistants draw the sand painting, letting tiny colored grains of sand, ocher or charcoal trickle between the index and middle finger of their hands. Sand paintings are drawn on preceding nights as well, but the most powerful is created on the final night.

The *'iikááh* (sand painting or, more literally, "enter and go") opens the door to the powerful worlds where the Earth, Sun, Moon, Mountains, and Holy People first appeared. Those creative forces enter the world once more through the picture. As soon as the painting is completed, the powerful objects are carried inside and placed carefully around the sand painting. This is a moment of great promise but also of great danger, for these mighty forces are present in a strong way. The moment need not last long to have an effect. The girl is quickly led along a pollen path prepared for her and seated at the very center of the powerful picture with her face turned toward the east. The singer and others sing prayers and chants over her. She is sprinkled with moisture, and her body and thoughts fill completely with the revitalizing power of the holy figures. At the same time, the painted dry figures draw out of her the *nayéé'*, the sickening forces that block her good health, and absorb them into the sand. When she finally stands and comes outside to breathe air from each direction, the colored sands will be swept up, carried outside, and scattered to the winds. Outside, the song and dance continue through the night until the final prayer near dawn. The girl will go back inside and stay in the *hogan* for four more nights, keeping to herself and watching carefully what she says, does and eats.

The rite of healing that returns one to the center of a reality full of meaning, finds expression in the religiosity of the whole world.

2
THE CRADLE OF HISTORY: MULTIPLE SOURCES OF NAVAJO KNOWLEDGE

The Navajo, originally nomads, exhibited in the course of their history a flexibility and a capacity for absorption of cultural elements derived from other peoples. These characteristics have brought them to cultural forms reworked in original and highly creative ways. The emphasis on dynamism and continuous regenerative movement of existence are fundamental attitudes of the Navajo. This scene of the passing of tradition to the younger generation depicts the ability of the Navajo to bring together the realities of the modern world with the deep roots that are embedded in the rich soil of sacredness.

The old *hataalii* who healed the girl is visiting her school to explain Navajo religious history to the children in the class. To make his point, he holds up a traditional cradleboard. This is an infant carrier used by Navajo mothers to hold their children on their backs as they walk. He shows the students that the cradleboard is made of several different pieces, each flap necessary to support and mold the child as it grows. One large panel represents the training received in the home; a second long panel stands for the formal, traditional education that comes from ceremonial experience over the course of a lifetime. There are also cross-braces that show how other, new kinds of knowledge have been integrated into the Navajo worldview over several generations. These changing influences have their origin in the history of Navajo contacts with foreigners. The Navajos, the *hataalii* points out, have always been eager to learn whatever can be useful from many sources.

The *hataalii* points to the cross-straps that hold the cradleboard panels together and explains that Spanish Catholicism and Anglo-American Christianity have also affected Navajo religious thought. Also, more recently, the Native American Church, which centers its services on the eating of the sacred *peyote* plant, is being adopted by some Navajos in ways that adapt it to the traditional ceremonial system.

The old singer speaks calmly to the children about all these things. He concludes by saying that one additional form of religious knowledge has always been important and available to Navajos at every turn. He points to the headpiece that holds the child's cradleboard against the head of its mother: "This represents transcendent knowledge. Navajos have the ability to be instructed directly by the supernatural beings that dwell within the sky and the landscape (such as the four sacred mountains in Navajo territory), and in the major features of the universe (such as the Sun, Moon, Wind and Stars), as well as in human visions or dreams. All these forms of religious knowledge, even if they pull in different directions, work together to cradle growing Navajos and shape their experience of the world."

Navajo ancestors crossed from Asia to the American continent and must have settled in western Canada, where other Athabascan speakers are now found. At some time between the 10th and 11th centuries the Navajos, who were nomadic hunters, moved to the southwest United States. By 1525, archaeologists tell us, they were in their current homeland—the Four Corners area of the Colorado plateau, where Arizona, New Mexico, Utah and Colorado intersect. From their immediate neighbors, the Apache and Pueblo peoples, they learned a great deal, including farming techniques, religious ceremonies and graphic religious art. They also learned from their Ute, Paiute, and Havasupai neighbors. From contacts with Spanish- and English-speaking Europeans, the Navajos encountered Christian ideas and practices as well as other things, such as the horse, which altered their way of life once again. In the late 1700s and early 1800s, the Navajo population flourished, centering their livelihood on the herding of sheep and goats, and using newly acquired skills of weaving to trade goods with Europeans and Mexicans. But contact with Europeans also brought untold suffering for the Navajos and their neighbors. After the United States took control of the southwest territory in 1846, there was increasing conflict amongst the Navajos, other settlers, and the military. In 1863, Navajo crops and homes were systematically destroyed by Colonel Kit Carson and his soldiers, operating under orders from the U.S. government. Reduced to desperation, the Navajos left the land prepared for them by their divine beings and endured the catastrophic Long Walk, a painful journey of displacement to Fort Sumner, 300 miles away in New Mexico. There, the Navajos were concentrated in a camp. They developed new ceremonies to pray for their freedom. Food shortage and disease hit the Navajos hard between 1864 and 1868, when they were released from detention by the U.S. Congress. This devastation took a toll on their religious life. An important theme in Navajo religious philosophy to this day is the question of restarting and reviving life in the face of the certain death of individuals and the final extinction of the Navajo people.

At the time of their release from captivity and return to 24,000 square miles of government-allotted land in 1868, their number had dwindled to 5,000-7,000 people. Hard economic times followed until commercial herding, weaving (learned from the Pueblo), and silversmithing (acquired from Mexicans) pulled some groups out of economic depression. Those rays of hope were dashed in 1930, however, when the entire U.S. economy fell into depression and the U.S. government implemented the Stock Reduction Act to limit the size of grazing herds. The commercial herding of sheep and goats no longer paid. A central theme in all the Navajo ceremonies performed over the last century has been to reproduce, increase, and thrive. Today there are more than 200,000 Navajos. Their sacred land is threatened by the presence of hazardous wastes and mining excavations. Employment on and around the reservations is hard to find and most workers are employed in public service fields such as health and education, or in government work. Others have migrated to cities such as Los Angeles and Kansas City to find work.

3
"DINÉ BIKÉYAH" NAVAJO COUNTRY

For the Navajo the whole earth is alive, the cradle of a connection between mortals and the forces of nature, animated by immortal "inner forms" with human features. Places and stories are associated with these forms, which transformed their landscape into a homeland.

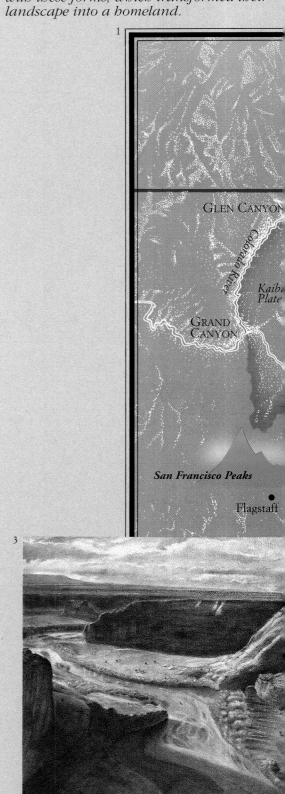

1. The land of the Navajo "Diné Bikéyah," with the sacred mountains, Blanca Peak, associated with the color white, to the East; Mount Taylor, with blue, to the South; San Francisco Peaks, with yellow, to the West; Hesperus Peak, with black, to the North. The darker gray area indicates the actual boundaries of the Navajo Reservation; the lighter area at the center represents the Hopi Reservation. The small map (bottom right) locates the area in the United States. **2.** Monument Valley. It is only one of the many different settings in this area. **3.** The Canyon de Chelly: one of the most fertile areas. Among the Navajo, agricultural interests are not very strong, but the correlation between agriculture and the celestial constellations symbolizes the harmony between earth and sky.

2

Colorado River

UTAH

COLORADO

Hesperus Peak

Blanca Peak

Sangre de Cristo Mts.

MONUMENT VALLEY

Aghaala

Kayenta

San Juan River

Carrizo Mts.

Lukachukai

Tsaile

Rough Rock

Chuska Mts.

ba City

Chinle

Piñon

CANYON DE CHELLY

HOPI RESERVATION

Mount Huerfano

Gobernador Knob

TAOS

Ganado

Saint Michaels

CHACO CANYON

Santa Fe

Rio Grande River

Gallup

San Mateo Mts.

Little Colorado River

Mount Taylor

Zuni Mts.

Grants

Albuquerque

Winslow

Holbrook

LAGUNA

ARIZONA

NEW MEXICO

UTAH

COLORADO

Pacific Ocean

California

ARIZONA

NEW MEXICO

MEXICO

13

SACRED SPACE ON THE EARTH'S SURFACE

To restore their health, revive their existence, and live life to the fullest, Navajos have constantly returned to the home territory set out and sanctified for them by the Holy People who created the world. The spatial design of that world holds great meaning and power. The special ceremonial house, such as the one where the young girl was healed, is called *hogan*, which literally means "home place." Understanding the *hogan* helps us learn about the sacred space of the Navajos because the building is a miniature model of the space designed by the gods and it contains all that is essential in the Navajo world. The four forked posts that mark the main points of the *hogan* are images of the four sacred mountains on which the vault of the sky rests like the roof of a *hogan*. The sacred mountains were fashioned of soil carried up from the under-

2. An uninhabited "hogan" attests to the details of construction: solid logs of pine, which at one time were covered by a layer of clay, mark out its profile, full of symbolic evocations. These are so strongly felt by the Navajo that even today, at the Navajo Community College, the directional divisions of the "hogan" have been used to plan the layout of the campus, with its various buildings for student activities.

1. The directional divisions of the "hogan"—associated with mythical beings, colors, mountains, and the four directions—are more than a division of space: they are living forces like knowledge, wisdom, struggle, the forces that challenge human beings and to which they turn in prayer.

N

Hesperus Peak (darkness)

North recess

Blanca Peak (dawn)

San Francisco Peaks (sunset)

W

West recess   hearth   East recess   entrance

South recess

Mount Taylor (midday)

S

1

Colorado River

Black Me

2

San Francisco Peaks

Little Colorado River

world in the medicine bundle of the First Man. Those clots of soil were mixed with variously colored jewels and light (white shells in the east, turquoise in the south, yellow mollusks in the west, and black jet in the north). The mixing of soil from the female earth with the colored jewels (thought to be drops of dew from the masculine sky) represents reproduction. The four mixtures are then placed in the four quarters of the Navajo world. Each mountain is something of a *hogan* in its own right, for placed within each one is a life-giving force that breathes and speaks. The sacred mountains are still the sources of sacred soils and objects used for ceremonies as well as the homes of vitalizing winds, colors, divine beings, stages of life, emotions, times of day, and so on. When walking in the *hogan*, or when naming or praying to the four

sacred mountain beings, it is important to follow the clockwise path of the Sun. To the east, where the Sun enters the world, is Blanca Peak, the home of dawn and of Talking God, a male. The *hogan* opens to the east, just as the world opens to the reappearance of the Sun's light each day. To the south is Mount Taylor, home of the blue sky of full daylight. In the west one finds San Francisco Peaks, home of the yellow twilight and of Calling God, a male being. Talking God on the East Mountain and Calling God on the West Mountain are leading chiefs: they provide knowledge, and they can tell the future. They guide and oversee human life and they also keep the sky informed about earthly matters. To the north is Hesperus Peak, where darkness lives. The Navajo world and the Navajo ceremonial house are similar because they were both constructed by the *diyin dine'é*, the Holy People, when they first emerged onto the surface of the Earth. In fact, one could say that the *hogan* they created when they first emerged was the world itself. Inside the roof of the first *hogan*, these holy designers placed key constellations, and so it is today that the sky, the vaulted roof of the world-*hogan*, is marked by those same stars. In fact, the central fire of the ceremonial *hogan* marks the place where the pole star Polaris sits in the sky, around which the stars circle. The *hogan* is a

order of space has played a vital role in Navajo ceremonies and knowledge ever since. Using the design of sacred space, Navajos are able to classify and give life to other elements of their life and so sustain and extend the order of creation. It is not surprising that Navajos return to center themselves in this sacred space when they are sick, displaced, fighting in foreign wars, or in need of increased vitality and wisdom.

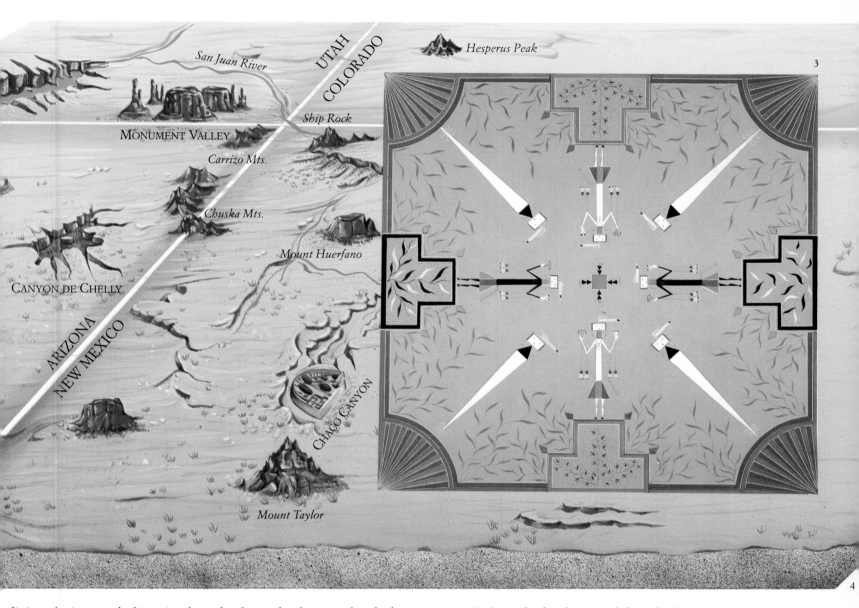

living being, exhaling its breath through the smoke hole where prayers rise to the sky.

It should come as no surprise that Earth itself is viewed as a living *hogan*, for it is believed that the world and the first *hogan* were divinely planned for the *hózhóójí* Blessingway ceremony that First Man, First Woman and the Holy People performed as soon as they emerged onto the surface of the Earth. That is why this special order of sacred space is so powerful; it represents the Holy People's first ideas and their first acts in this world. The creation of the *hogan* was designed as a ritual to bring about greater clarity, order and knowledge; the Holy People set objects in their proper places, breathed life into them through ritual actions and chants, and so instructed future people about their meaning. The ritual

3. 4. In the background that displays several prominent characteristics of Navajo territory, a watercolor reproduces a sand painting used in the Mountainway ceremony. The words sung in this ritual reflect an intense and affective participation with nature, a testimony to the profound experience that binds the Navajo to their land. In this watercolor, from the four corner fans, which are signs of the rainbow, rise the white figures of the spirits of the mountains heading toward the center. They seem to circle the other characters against a backdrop of luxuriant vegetal elements.

THE FIVE WORLDS AND SACRED TIME

1. The Arizona sky in the Navajo Tribal Park of Monument Valley, traversed by a great rainbow. It manifests to the world, inhabited by mankind, all the colors that make the land luminous, cloaking it with the supreme beauty that the Navajo identify as a manifestation of its sacredness.

The history of the Navajo people unfolds not merely from one century to another, but also from one world to another. Navajo history descends deep into the Earth to include a series of underworlds. The *diyin dine'é* lived in all these worlds, one after another. The world on the surface, in which Navajos live today, is the fifth world to exist. The four underworlds, where life and death unfolded before the present world, are stacked one below the other and go down as far as time can be imagined. The worlds are pictured as containers, like baskets or bowls of colored crystal. The heart of the ceremonial system, *hózhóójí*, leads back into the time of earlier worlds. That is how life in the earlier underworlds is known: through the knowledge gained in ceremonies, especially *hózhóójí*.

Each earlier world is represented by a different color. Black is the lowest, then come the red, blue, and yellow worlds, before you enter this world—a world of multiple colors. The worlds are thought to be stacked, one within the other. *Nihodilgil,* the first and lowest world, contains all the others within itself. *Nihodilgil* is an obscure and vague place—a jet-black world where darkness is layered on darkness. The darkness of *Nihodilgil* encompasses the creative darkness at work within the magic medicine bundle of the First Man. First Man's medicine bundle is the source of every-thing that has happened below, above, or on the Earth and in all creative moments of all creative ages. The many darknesses of *Nihodilgil*, lying one on top of the other, came together to produce something new.

It is believed that each world ended in destruction through flood, fire, or chaos and, in haste, the Holy People scampered to the next world. There, First Man's repeated actions changed the vague sounds, soils, and mists of the preceding worlds into increasingly clear and colorful creatures of the later worlds.

Key spaces became markers of time. The five worlds themselves represent different ages of creation. In addition, the four light tones marking the horizons of space in each direction (white in the east, blue in the south, yellow in the west, and black in the north) also tell the time of day (dawn, full day, twilight, darkness) and the phase of the life cycle (birth, mature life, old age, death). These cycles also correspond to rotating patterns of color, direction, emotion, and size; they combine with other markers, such as the Sun, Moon, seasons, and stars, to produce a regulated world of order and precision. Following the order and space created by these markers, things like day and night, summer and winter, rainy and wet times, birth and death, and plant and animal cycles come and go regularly within the ceremonial calendar.

2. The stories of the origin of all things depict man's spiritual search. For the Navajo these stories are a 'holy book' which generates everyday life. Here the underworlds are represented, which in Navajo stories constitute the initial situation, before the earth was inhabited by humans. On the one hand, the inhabitants (insects, animals, or the original men) ascend tirelessly, leaving disaster behind them. On the other hand, in a progressive growth, each world is more harmonious than the previous one. As the beings become increasingly human, life itself takes a multicolored form, thus conquering the darkness.

3. After crossing through successive worlds, the beings who emerged onto the surface of the multicolored world, must face new dangers, but the earth will replenish itself with plants, food, and medicine for people and animals.

2

17

EMERGING AND PLACING: THE PROCESS OF CREATION

Navajo creation stories describe the wanderings of the first beings, called *diyin dine'é*, or Holy People. They traveled through the underworlds and emerged onto the Earth's surface. In the first underworld there was, in the beginning, no movement, no light, no sound. Formless Mist People breathed and sighed in the dark, moving invisibly without purpose or direction. Under the blanket of eastern darkness in the First World, Black Mist and White Mist united to produce First Man and white corn. Under the cover of western darkness, Blue Mist and Yellow Mist coupled to form First Woman and yellow corn. (The importance of corn to the Navajo is clear, as part of the very first creation.)

Four dark oceans pooled on the edges of the world. Groups of invisible winds came together and fought until the chiefs of the four oceans became upset with their behavior. The four ocean chiefs made the waters rise to flood the world. In a panic, the winds flew away (in the form of dark flying ants, dragonflies, colored beetles, bats, and locusts) and emerged through a hole into a higher world.

Guided by voices and winds, First Man and First Woman made the upward journey through time, passing through red, blue and yellow worlds. In each of the worlds, they encountered objects of great value and great danger. During the voyage, sighing gave way to specific words, names, and songs; creatures multiplied; their colors and forms became more distinct. First Man, First Woman, and their companions populated each world in turn until some catastrophe brought that world to an end and sent them scrambling into the next higher world. They crawled like insects along an upward-twirling vine or spiraled their way through narrow passages tunneled for them by the winds. In their baskets and bundles, the *diyin dine'é* carried powerful reminders of every world they left behind.

Throughout this eventful climb, First Man repeated the same process that created him: "covering" substances found in the earlier worlds with colored sheets, blankets, or skins. Sometimes he sprinkled the items with fluid or dew; sometimes he paired them with another substance. In the dark of their wrappings, the hidden substances reproduced new ones or were transformed and brought alive with wind, breath, and song. Assisted by other Holy People, First Man would then unwrap the newly created beings, just as he unwrapped his powerful medicine bundle containing all knowledge, and place the dazzling creations in their proper setting. That is why the Navajos call these creations *niilyáii*, meaning "the things that were placed" (or created) by the Holy People.

In the same way, in the first moments after coming up onto the Earth's surface, when the ground had nearly dried from the flood, First Man opened the wraps of his medicine bundle and displayed to the other *diyin dine'é* items brought from the previous worlds. He had wrapped them in several layers of sheets now associated with the major light tones (white shell in the east, turquoise in the south, yellow in the west, and black in the north). By displaying and "placing" the

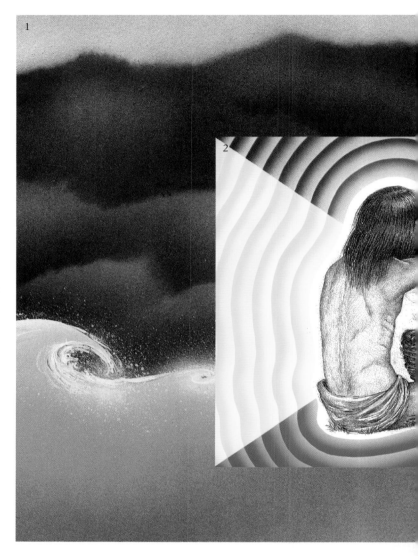

1. 2. Against the background of the primordial waters that had submerged the world, we see First Man as he transforms the amorphous mists originating from the primordial darkness into the radiance of changing colors of the four cardinal directions: black to the North; blue to the South; white to the East; yellow to the West. This is the luminosity that is refracted into many colors, marking even the passage of time according to the days and the seasons.

3. The flowering plants in the desert speak with vivid color: life on earth blossoms from beings rich in beauty and power.

4. Ancient agricultural tools found near the Chaco region. The Navajo, coming from the North, adopted local cultivation techniques. Here we see digging sticks for planting corn, and, second from the top, the handle of a stone hoe. The earth, in the original Navajo stories, offers its fruits to those who work the land.

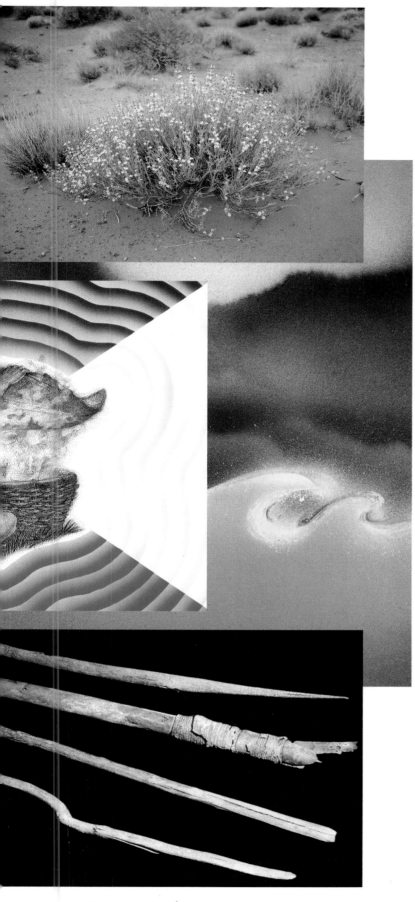

the fifth world at the horizons of the four different directions. The world of the Navajo, like the life-changing basket the *diyin dine'é* brought with them, was placed between these sheets of colored light and so is in a constant state of change.

At the first gathering of Holy People in the new world, First Man was host and ceremonial singer. Under his direction, the *diyin dine'é* also placed materials into a basket, which functioned as a kind of *hogan*. The basket was covered completely with sheets made of the inner forms of the major colors (pairs of colors lay on top of one other with the basket in between them). As the *diyin dine'é* sang the *hózhóójí* chants of Blessingway, the material inside the basket changed form and came to life with the breezes and breath that entered with the song. This is how First Man and the Holy People created Earth, Sky, Sun, Moon, and various animals. The Navajo repeat the *hózhóójí* first celebrated on the Earth's surface to continue the process of creation.

Toward the end of his creative career, First Man produced his most beautiful creations. They were a young couple of exquisite beauty named *Sa'a naghái ashkii* and *Bik'e hózhó at'ééd*. These are the beings that give life to the Sky and the Earth, and so energize the whole world. They are the final product of the medicine bundle that brought life to the world. Everything that has life on Earth reflects their beauty and power.

Among the created beings, one deserves a special mention. Her name is *Asdzáá nádlehíí*, or Changing Woman. At one point along the journey up to the new world, men and women became separated by a great river, with each then living on a different riverbank. The generation of new life came to a standstill. During this time, *nayéé'* were born. The *nayéé'* are hideous creatures who cause disease and misery. They nearly wiped out the Holy People. To correct this, First Man created Changing Woman. He pointed with his medicine bundle to her birthplace and enlisted the help of First Woman, Earth and Sky, and *Ch'óol'í'í* (the mountain called Gobernador Knob on which Changing Woman was born). First Man taught Changing Woman what he knew. When she was grown, Changing Woman gave birth to twins, who were fathered by the Sun. The twins were named *Nayéé' neezghání* (Monster Slayer) and *Tóbájishchíní* (Born for Water). They battled the *nayéé'* and defeated them so that the *diyin dine'é* could live in the world. Today, the twins help sick patients by journeying to the underworlds to fight off the *nayéé'* who afflict them.

Eventually First Man passed his powerful medicine bundle over to Changing Woman. With the life-giving powers of the winds and of *Sa'a naghái* and *Bik'e hózhó*, Changing Woman used the bundle to bring the Navajo to life by transforming several substances, including rubbings from her own skin and other matters such as corn, colored jewels, water or dew, and mountain soil. She also used the bundle and the *hózhóójí* ceremonial process to make sheep and the 12 corn and vegetable spirits that sustain the Navajo. Changing Woman continues to work for the good of the Navajo people. In the spring, she has the form of a young girl; in the winter she changes into the form of a barren old woman.

Navajos tell many different versions of these stories; each version is designed to help them understand the importance of their world and how it came to be.

contents of his bundle, he altered their form, showing the power of the *hózhóójí* ceremony he was enacting. This is how the prominent features and powers of the surface world were created. For example, the vague surrounding mists from which First Man himself was made in the first world eventually became the light tones that now wrap themselves around

HOLY WIND: FROM THE ONE TO THE MANY

In Navajo tradition, the process of creation involves wind entering all beings in the world and breathing life into them. There is only one wind, *Nílch'i*, though *Nílch'i* can have many names. Different winds come from *Nílch'i*, and these smaller winds may be named for places, directions, size and rotation, effects and experiences. *Nílch'i*, the birthplace of all wind, is the one life force that already existed at the very first moment of creation. In that first dark and invisible world, the wind gave life and movement to formless mists and gave knowledge about this life to the Holy People. Wind was the breath that sighed forth from the first mists of light in the underworld, guiding and leading the clouds toward their places on the horizons: dawn in the east, blue sky in the south, yellow twilight in the west, and jet-black darkness in the north. Various winds called out to the Holy People and guided them on their upward path, leading them into new worlds as well as into knowledge and wisdom. Whenever First Man covered substances and chanted aloud, wind entered into them to transform them and bring them to life. Wind emerged onto the Earth's surface with the Holy People. Wind is the force behind the creation of so many different forms of life, light and knowledge. Every form of creation, great or small, has a wind inside that can call out to humans and teach them. When human beings were created, wind entered their bodies, leaving the marks of its passing on the whirled patterns found on the skin of their hands, fingers, feet, and heads. The distinctive patterns of hair and feathers are the marks the wind leaves on each different species of animals when it brings them to life. And when each new life is conceived, wind brings breath, guidance and protection to the new creature that emerges.

A tiny wind, called Wind's Child, is placed in the fold of a human being's ear to whisper the truth and to become the basis of each individual conscience.

Wind not only brings life for the first time, but also purifies and refreshes life from time to time. In the girl's healing ceremony described earlier, the wind not only animated the *hogan* and all the powerful figures in the sand painting as well as the songs and bodies of the dancers, but at the end of the ceremony, the wind also scattered the sands and, with them, the forces that made her sick.

The wind, which for the Navajo is the source of life, movement and activity, has often human attributes. The wind, which makes voice and communication possible, provides energy for the vital interchange among the various components of the world and enlivens the inner forms of beings. These forms reside in the depths of every phenomenon, plant and animal, rendering them alive, and in their turn capable of giving life. This picture shows how the sand of the painting used during the ceremony is entrusted to the wind. The wind reminds humans not to forget the evocative power of sand-painted images that come to us from a mythical world suspended in space and time.

FATHER SKY, MOTHER EARTH: PAIRED OPPOSITES

Life in the Navajo world comes from pairings. At every point, opposite forces constantly combine with one another in helpful ways to produce fruitful life. The Navajos call this universal process *alkéé naa'aashii*. Underneath paired blankets of darkness, the colored mists from the corners of the world joined with one another, two by two, to produce the original couple, First Man and First Woman. The basket First Man used to transform pairs of substances brought from the underworlds was set between pairs of sheets, one above and one below the basket. In the same way, the Navajo land (a place of constant life-sustaining changes) is set between two pairs of sacred mountains, which are always joined together: east with south and west with north. Inside the light that wraps each horizon lives a pair of *diyin dine'é*, one male and one female, who give life to the mountain in that quarter. Within each of the *diyin dine'é* are *nílch'i* winds that pair with one another. Every human being is a combination of paired winds, one female wind from the mother and one male wind from the father. Many of the paired conditions of Navajo life take their character from Changing Woman, who is young and fruitful in the summer, but old and barren during the winter. Even birth and death complement one another in essential ways.

The most important pair of opposites is Father Sky and Mother Earth. Father Sky and Mother Earth complement one another perfectly, like the two halves of a sliced, ripe melon. All life in heaven and on earth unfolds within them. In sand paintings, Father Sky is drawn with the Sun, Moon, and starry constellations of the night sky on his body; the Milky Way moves across his chest and outstretched arms. In the center of Mother Earth's body is a gourd marking the spot where the Holy People emerged from the underworlds. The gourd holds fluid left over from the flood. From her body grow the important plants used in food and ceremonies: tobacco, squash, beans, and corn. Father Sky and Mother Earth are given life by the young couple that lives and breathes within them—a pair of extraordinary beauty named *Sa'a naghái ashkii* and *Bik'e hózhó at'ééd*. Changing Woman, who created the first human couple, is often described as the child of *Sa'a naghái ashkii* and *Bik'e hózhó at'ééd*. Their relationship is constantly changing and yielding new, fruitful life. For this reason, *Sa'a naghái ashkii* and *Bik'e hózhó at'ééd* are the model and inspiration for all pairs in the universe.

1. A view from Monument Valley. The land of the Navajo is marked with signs of the same wind which is so important in their spirituality. It hearkens back to the idea of dynamic power, a transforming and perpetual movement that informs the Navajo worldview.

1

9. A Navajo woman watches the work at an open mine that nearly encroaches on her home. The imbalance and trauma provoked by abusive mining practices are displayed in this image.

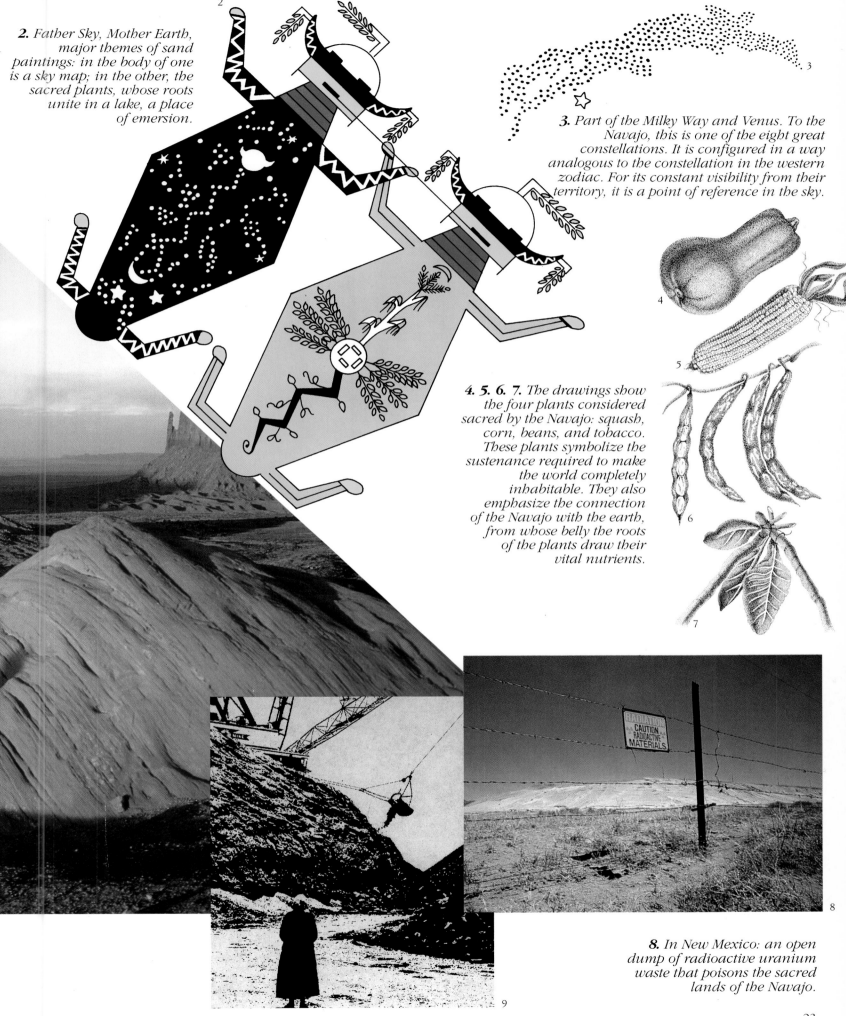

2. *Father Sky, Mother Earth, major themes of sand paintings: in the body of one is a sky map; in the other, the sacred plants, whose roots unite in a lake, a place of emersion.*

3. *Part of the Milky Way and Venus. To the Navajo, this is one of the eight great constellations. It is configured in a way analogous to the constellation in the western zodiac. For its constant visibility from their territory, it is a point of reference in the sky.*

4. 5. 6. 7. *The drawings show the four plants considered sacred by the Navajo: squash, corn, beans, and tobacco. These plants symbolize the sustenance required to make the world completely inhabitable. They also emphasize the connection of the Navajo with the earth, from whose belly the roots of the plants draw their vital nutrients.*

8. *In New Mexico: an open dump of radioactive uranium waste that poisons the sacred lands of the Navajo.*

23

9
WHOLENESS, HARMONY, AND BEAUTY: "SA'A NAGHÁI BIK'E HÓZHÓ"

Sa'a naghái Bik'e hózhó is the goal of Navajo life and the most important theme in Navajo religious thinking. The phrase has two parts and many related meanings. *Sa'a naghái* can mean "in old age walking" and brings to mind the image of a long life, full of enriching experiences. *Bik'e hózhó* can mean "his trail beautiful," showing the kind of happiness, perfection, and order that can be gained by humans in an ideal environment. When spoken together, the two halves of the phrase indicate a continuous cycle of walking one's path from beginning to end, repeating the cycles of life, of planting and harvesting, of celebrating ceremonies. The cycle includes opposite moments: full growth and maturity, but also a return to youth, or to the freshness of creation at its first appearance. *Sa'a naghái Bik'e hózhó* refers to the completeness that comes when, in the course of this constant and never-ending journey, as cycles occur and recur, pairs of opposites achieve a vital, harmonious whole greater than the sum of their parts. The reason the universe exists is to create the beauty that results when the inner forms of the Sky and Earth unite to form *Sa'a naghái Bik'e hózhó*, and this is also the purpose of each of the world's parts. *Sa'a naghái Bik'e hózhó* is the goal of Navajo ceremonies and the outcome that inspired the actions of First Man and the Holy People. *Sa'a naghái Bik'e hózhó* also refers to the medicine bundle and its contents, and to the life-giving qualities that dwell within the special objects "placed" in *hózhóójí*, the Blessingway ceremony. In addition to these meanings, *Sa'a naghái Bik'e hózhó* is also used in everyday speech to mean completeness, the condition of healthy, living beings.

The illustration represents the construction of a modern "hogan." The Navajo each day try to live out the fact that knowledge of the origin of all things can confer a harmonious existence on the present, when that knowledge is applied with awareness to the acts of living. The "hogan," in its role of cosmic model, gives meaning to everyday space, and well represents this conviction, even in the building phase, when the unity of the group's members demonstrates their shared fidelity to their origins.

TESTIMONY

GREY MUSTACHE SPEAKS

"Children, I want you to know how I think. I'm very old, Grandchildren, Children, and what I have to offer you is getting scarce. The old people's knowledge is that by which one looks up and sees the world after the sun has risen. By means of knowledge, one makes one's way through the day from the time the first light is seen in the East until the darkness rises and finally the world becomes dark. At that time, one can no longer see.

"And so it is that when one doesn't know the traditions, one has nothing to light one's way. It is as though one lived with a covering on one's eyes, as if one lived being deaf and blind. Yet when one knows the traditions, one has vision to see as far as Black Mountain and beyond, to see all the way to where the land meets the ocean. It's as though one's vision becomes as good as that. I long for you to realize what it is that your ancestors had, and how it is that some of us old people still live our lives.

"If you would only come to know our words and would take the time to think them over, you would come to know that they were true and valuable. These teachings are of a kind that you would someday want to use in teaching your own children. But hardly any of you will listen to us anymore, even though there are now so many of you. And so it is up to those few of you who do want to learn. You will never be alone. You'll learn one thing after another and the old people will help you. Then, the more you learn, the more you'll be able to tie things together and understand.

"And so it is up to those of you who are really interested to listen and to make sense for yourselves of what we say. Then you will come to be respected and sought after for advice. . . people will think of you as a living, sparking fire.

"And then here's another thing. Others will speak of the dead in the past tense, but you knowledgeable ones will say 'So and so says this,' even though the teller is dead. Though the person had died, the knowledge has been passed on and is alive. . ."

Statement taken down and translated by Allen Manning and Frank Harvey and published in John R. Farella, *The Main Stalk: A Synthesis of Navajo Philosophy* (London and Tucson: University of Arizona Press, 1984; third printing 1993, p. 24-25).

A Navajo boy watches the boundless horizon of Monument Valley. The wisdom that comes from his spiritual heritage alights on this incomparable scene and seems to echo in the words of Grey Mustache. The mountains, the sky, and the colors of the earth are revered as personal calls made to each young Navajo and living reminders capable of creating a fruitful rapport with a living tradition. As a Native American educator said a few years ago "The religion of the Navajo is being a Navajo."

GLOSSARY

Words in CAPITALS are cross references

Alkéé naa'aashii A process of continuously cycling through the differences and complementary oppositions present in all realities, thus giving them vibrant, changing life. Through this process opposites are united: birth and death, youth and old age, increase and demise, hunger and satiety, love and hate, weakness and strength, night and day, winter and summer, work and rest, and especially male and female.

Apache A tribe of Native Americans who are neighbors to the Navajo.

Athabascan The family of languages to which the Navajo language belongs. Other Athabascan speakers live in western Canada.

Bii'gistíín The INNER FORM of a reality which animates it and gives it life and purpose.

Bik'e hózhó at'ééd See SA'A NAGHÁI ASHKII and BIK'E HÓZHÓ AT'ÉÉD.

Blanca Peak (Sis Najiní) Marks an eastern point of the Navajo world.

Chahalhéél The darkness that dwells on the northern horizon and one of the four mists in the first world.

Changing Woman Created the Navajo and sustains their life in the world today.

Diyin dine'é Holy People. The first beings to exist. They lived in previous worlds now located in the underworlds and emerged to the earth's surface over time, creating realities along the way. The terms also refer to natural phenomena such as rain, sun, thunder, and wind.

Dzil leezh Literally, "Mountain Soil." The name of the magic medicine bundle of First Man and used in the HÓZHÓÓJÍ. It contains soil and jewels from the mountains of the cardinal directions (that is the earth's flesh moistened by the dew of the sky), which are the source of breath and life on earth, wrapped in unwounded buckskin.

First Man and First Woman They led the Holy People on their journey from the underworlds. First Man directed the creative transformation and placement of creatures.

Hataalii Singer or chanter. One who possesses special knowledge of ceremonies, sand painting, diagnoses, and completion (cure) exercises.

Hayoolkáál The white light of dawn that wraps the eastern horizon and one of the mists that inhabited the first world.

Hesperus Peak (Dibé Nitsaa) Marks a northern point of the Navajo world.

Hogan From *hoo-* "place," and *-ghan* "home." A special ceremonial building which contains in miniature all the essential features and forces of the Navajo world. It is the place of the ceremonial transformations which continue the process of creation.

Hózhó A common way of referring to SA'A NAGHÁI BIK'E HÓZHÓ.

Hózhó ntséskees Right thinking. Since thought is creative, one must cultivate the best quality thoughts so as to draw toward oneself desirable experiences that affect the quality of one's life.

Hózhóójí The Blessingway ceremony, which continues the creative process by which First Man transforms realities, gives them life and purpose, and places them on display in the world.

'Iikááh Sandpainting. A place of passage where powerful beings come and go and where entry is made to the underworlds.

Inner forms Natural objects and human beings possess inner forms that are animated by the Wind and exist independently from those beings they occupy. Navajo rituals are carried out to interact with the inner forms of the Holy People.

Medicine Bundle A pouch containing powerful items and placed for display during ceremonies. First Man brought substances from the underworld in his medicine bundle and transformed them creatively when he displayed them in his ceremonial actions. Changing Woman took over the use of First Man's medicine bundle and uses it on behalf of human beings.

Mount Taylor (Tsoodzil) Marks a southern point of the Navajo world.

Nahagha Ceremony.

Nahinii'na Something that comes back to animated life. The term can refer, for example, to patients who undergo healing ceremonies.

Náhodetl'izh Blue associated with the southern horizon during the height of day and a mist existing in the first world.

Náhotsoi Evening twilight. The yellow associated with the western horizon after sunset and a mist of the first and lowest underworld.

Nayéé' A monstrous being or other negative condition that prevents life from being lived to its fullest. *Nayéé'* are responsible for physical sickness, weakness, poverty, fear, and sadness.

Niilyáii "Things that were placed." The realities that were created and set in place by First Man and the Holy People.

Nílch'í Holy wind. The force that animates all life.

Nílch'í biyázhí Child Wind. The small winds that help the Holy People know the future or hear at great distances by whispering in their ears.

Pueblo A Native American tribe who are neighbors of the Navajo.

Sa'a naghái ashkii and **Bik'e hózhó at'ééd** The two young beautiful ones who were First Man's most exquisite creations. They are the inner animating life-force of the sky and earth.

Sa'a naghái Bik'e hózhó The completeness and all-inclusive beauty or harmony which is the goal of life. The phrase can be literally translated as "in old age walking, his trail beautiful" or "according to the ideal may restoration be achieved" and refers to the continuous recurrence of the completion of the cycle of life and maturity. The phrase can refer to the power of First Man's medicine bundle and the inner forms of the Earth and Sky combined, as well as to all things created and placed during the HÓZHÓÓJÍ. In everyday speech it refers to the beauty of the landscape, good health, and harmonious relations with others.

San Francisco Peaks (Dook'o'oosłííd) Mountain marking a western point of the Navajo world.

BIBLIOGRAPHY

BENALLY, HERBERT JOHN, "Diné Bo'ohoo'aah Bindii'a': A Navajo Philosophy of Learning," *Diné Be'iiná: Journal of Navajo Life*, vol. 1, n. 1 (1987).

——, "Spiritual Knowledge for a Secular Society," *Tribal College Journal*, vol. 4, n. 1 (1992).

——, "Navajo Philosophy of Learning and Pedagogy," *Journal of Navajo Education*, vol. 12, n. 1 (Fall 1994): p. 23-31.

GRIFFIN-PIERCE, TRUDY, *Earth Is My Mother, Sky Is My Father*, Albuquerque: University of New Mexico Press, 1992.

HAILE, BERARD, *The Upward Moving Emergence Way*, Lincoln: University of Nebraska Press, 1981.

——, *Women versus Men: A Conflict of Navajo Emergence*, Lincoln: University of Nebraska Press, 1981.

HAILE, BERARD, MAUD OAKES, and LELAND C. WYMAN, *Beautyway: A Navaho Ceremonial*, Bollingen Series 53, New York: Pantheon Books, 1957.

McNELEY, JAMES KALE, (article on cradleboard), *Journal of Navajo Education*, vol. 12, n. 1 (Fall 1994).

——, *Holy Wind in Navajo Philosophy*, Tucson: University of Arizona Press, 1981.

REICHARD, GLADYS A., *Navajo Religion. A Study of Symbolism* (2nd edition), New York: Pantheon, 1970.

SULLIVAN, LAWRENCE E., *Native American Religions: North America*, Religion, History and Culture Series, New York: Macmillan, 1989.

WITHERSPOON, GARY, *Language and Art in the Navajo Universe*, Ann Arbor: The University of Michigan Press, 1977.

WYMAN, LELAND C., *Blessingway*, Tucson: University of Arizona Press, 1970.

——, *The Red Antway of the Navaho*, Museum of Navajo Ceremonial Art, Navajo Religion Series 5, Santa Fe: Museum of Navajo Ceremonial Art.

——, *The Windways of the Navaho*, Colorado Springs: Taylor Museum, 1962.

Index